1,401
More
Things That

P*SS
Me Off

1,401
More
Things That

P*SS
Me Off

I. M. (Still) Peeved

Ed Strnad

**Developed by
The Philip Lief Group, Inc.**

A Perigee Book

Perigee Books
are published by
The Putnam Publishing Group
200 Madison Avenue
New York, NY 10016

Library of Congress Cataloging-in-Publication Data
Peeved, I.M.
1,401 more things that p*ss me off / I.M. (Still) Peeved
(Ed Strnad) : developed by the Philip Lief Group, Inc.
    p.   cm.
ISBN 0-399-51823-1 (acid-free paper)
I. Philip Lief Group.   II. Title.   III. Title: 1,401 more things
that p*ss me off.   IV. Title: One thousand four hundred and one
more things that p*ss me off.
PN6162.P355   1993   93-3357 CIP
    818′.540208—dc20

Published by arrangement with
The Philip Lief Group, Inc.
6 West 20th Street, New York, NY 10011

Cover design by Richard Rossiter
Cover illustration by Ann Spinelli

Printed in the United States of America
  1   2   3   4   5   6   7   8   9   10

This book is printed on acid-free paper.
∞

Introduction

You're stuffed into your seat on an overbooked plane, en route to your annual visit with the planet's most grating relatives. To check your bubbling ire, you try to read the newspaper, a feat which, in coach class, requires the agility of an Olympic gymnast and the concentration of a yogi. After accidentally jabbing your elbow into the short-tempered bodybuilder to your left, you finally manage to unfurl the front page, which proclaims the New

World Order will bring about greener pastures and happier times for one and all. Before you can register the slightest smile, a baby screams so loud you think she is lodged in your skull, and you find yourself praying for Armageddon.

The lesson? There are more things to complain about in heaven and earth than can be found in a single book. That's why we've come up with *1401 More Things That P*ss Me Off,* some of which was written with your generous help. At the end of *1,401 Things That P*ss Me Off,* we invited our readers to speak their minds, to let off steam, to whine and moan until the cows came home. The response has been enormous—our floors are covered with sizzling lists of daily heartbreakers like split ends, leaky aquariums, midlife crises, and the death of Dr. Seuss. In sifting through all the submissions to find the tastiest peeves to combine with our own, we've hit upon a fundamental truth: we are a species that takes great pleasure in complaining.

While humorous, this is above all a self-help book, one filled with opportunities for personal growth. Learning that others also lament the loss of Dan Quayle as national punching bag will heal you. Your humanity will expand beyond recognition upon realizing how many share your agony over hearing yet another classic rock song transformed into a commercial for pantyhose. And think how soothing it will be to find you aren't the only one who contemplates homicide upon seeing a diner whip out her cellular phone at a restaurant.

Looking for guidance but can't find it in all those sappy tomes of inspiration? Kick back and get ready to sink your teeth into *1401 More Things That P*ss Me Off*, a communal kvetchfest that will leave you snickering at life's little atrocities.

burning the roof of your mouth on hot
   pizza

people who set off their own car alarms

cold fronts from Canada

when your helium balloon flies away

when someone has the same seat number as you on a full airplane

"put stamp here" instructions on
    envelopes

when you wake up and think it's Satur-
    day, but it's only Friday

when you wake up and think it's Sun-
    day, but it's already Monday

sitcom families that revel in their dys-
    functionalness

Socks, the First Cat

lip gloss that makes you look like you
smeared butter on your lips

group hugs

breaking a high heel outside and hob-
bling along like Igor in *Frankenstein*

having to wear a tie every day

resembling a criminal featured on
"America's Most Wanted"

psychological scars from parochial school

when you can see the ventriloquist's lips moving

newspaper thieves

gut-thumpingly loud car stereos that you can hear and feel from blocks away

getting a charley horse

misspelled graffiti

resumes with typographical errors

the fact that the world still spins mer-
    rily 'round after you die

people who say, "Howdy"

people who reply, "Doody"

people who quote Rush Limbaugh

being comedicly abused by a stand-up
    comic

parents of Little Leaguers

getting "the runs"

being unable to get past the first level
    of a videogame

people who say, "I may be stupid, but . . ."

that teeny-weeny spare tire in new cars

when your favorite rock song is recycled into an advertising jingle

realizing that beauty is only skin deep, but ugly's to the bone

everything you bring to a repair shop comes back with some new problem everything delicious is bad for you

everything tasteless is good for you

your car runs the same on regular or
    premium gas

zits on prom night

paycheck withholdings

hour-long waiting lines at amusement parks

the French

screaming babies on airplanes

screaming parents at airports

child-proof bottles

pushy panhandlers

April 15th

not knowing how the toaster knows
when the bread is done

dashboard warning lamps that come
on unexpectedly

adults who say, "bye-bye"

coworkers who take the last cup of
coffee, and don't make a new pot

coworkers who jam the copier, then
flee the scene of the crime

rain checks

back orders

no recognition for a job well done

when the rush hour lasts 5 hours

not having Dan Quayle to kick around
    anymore

laugh tracks

surprise birthday parties after thirty

midlife crises

when the radio calls your favorite songs, "the Moldy Oldies"

old people driving sports cars

X-rated movies with plots

bad-hair days

people who use cellular phones in restaurants

biographies of crazed killers for other
psychos to emulate

when the spare tire is flat too

locking your keys in the car

becoming addicted to nicotine patches

Perot in '96 bumper stickers

Quayle in '96 bumper stickers

people who read while driving

when the batteries leak and eat your
flashlight

why Wile E. Coyote bothers to chase
that scrawny Road Runner

food products with "Wiz" in their
names

discovering your inner child is a brat

being stumped by the TV Guide cross-
     word puzzle

when your baby calls the sitter
     "Mommy"

people who claim "I only watch PBS."

super-gluing your fingers together

hoaxes that you fall for

"My child's an honor student" bumper
stickers

starched shorts

ugly plastic surgeons

giving an interviewer a big phony
smile in order to get a job

when your parents call you their little
    "accident"

seeing   more   naked   pictures   of
    Madonna

when the toilet bowl overflows

people who call late-night radio talk-
    shows, natter on about nonsense
    and then say, "But that's not what
    I called about"

conspiracy theories

having to wear a beeper round-the-
  clock

phone solicitations during dinner

working for a jerk

celebrities who are famous because of
  whom they married

forgetting the combination to your
  locker

shirt labels that irritate the nape of
    your neck

Rolexes

after washing your hands and face, you
    find the restroom's out of paper
    towels

pets that snore

getting mooned

brown nosers

uninsured motorists

gridlock

mumblers

spitters

knuckle crackers

finger poppers

lint pickers

cheek pinchers

collect callers

sulkers

whiners

———————————

pool sharks

vegetarians who wear leather shoes

die-hard Nixon supporters

when someone points out a word
     you've mispronounced

when someone points out a word
     you've misspelled

when someone makes scary faces at
  your baby

getting caught using an expired supermarket coupon

deciding whether or not to eat the
  green potato chip

that MAD magazine isn't so funny
  anymore

when food you've swallowed goes
  down the wrong pipe

fans who do "the wave" too many
   times

the Twinkie defense

the lifestyles of the rich and famous

running to answer a phone that's ring-
   ing on TV

people who are still living in the '60s

people who are still living in the '70s

people who are still living in the '80s

when another car steals the parking
spot you're waiting for

people who say "you know?" at the
end of every sentence

"quirky" people

———————————————

excessive chutzpah

when you go out at night, get mugged,
    then are told, "Well, you asked
    for it"

when crooks go free on a technicality

lipstick on the milk carton

a car that blocks your driveway

people who say, "Got a problem with that?"

having to make idle conversation with your haircutter

when the alarm's still set come Saturday morning

shoes with taps

when someone behind you steps on the back of your shoe

loud parties next door on week nights

banks that take days to credit your account for deposits

when you leave behind your ATM receipt, and the next person laughs

when very old people win the lottery

able-bodied drivers parked in the handicapped spot

when your usual parking spot has been taken

hailstones "as big as golf balls" or bigger

regaining every pound lost on a diet

traffic jams that clear up as mysteriously as they began

a birthday cake with so many candles the smoke alarm goes off

having an argument with Customer
    Service

running over a skunk

the look you get when buying a box of
    Odor Eaters

grapefruits that always get you in
    the eye

being very short in a crowded elevator

that Edsels are valuable collectibles

when you rent a movie and it's on TV
that night

when you're almost asleep, the Captain announces you're flying over Toledo, Ohio

taking your shoes off in a Japanese restaurant when you're wearing smelly socks

playing telephone tag

catching yourself sounding just like
your mother

getting the finger from a child

celebrities who complain about how
hard it is to be rich and famous

big movie stars who shun the public

pineapple and bacon on pizzas

that more people can quote Ed Norton
than Shakespeare

the buttons on the remote control you
never use

movies mangled by the previous
renter's VCR

how you look and sound on videotape

drivers who speed up to prevent you
from passing them

spraying your armpits with hairspray

when your air fern suffocates

old folk remedies for colds that don't
    work but give you garlic-breath

single-passenger cars in the carpool
    lane

waking up with a headache

blonde jokes if you're blonde

"I'm not deaf, I'm ignoring you"
    bumper stickers

cutesy vanity plates

frozen dinners that look nothing like
    the picture on the box

when a toothpick splinters and lodges
    between your teeth

when the cat uses your plant for a
    litterbox

when your yo-yo smacks you in the
    skull

people who use up all the copier paper

cashiers who don't know how to make
    change

cash registers that talk to you

when the winner of the election is
announced before you've voted

annual employee performance reviews

all the haggling you have to do when
buying a car

appliances that break down over the
weekend

having to send a Christmas card
because somebody sent you one

eating Thanksgiving leftovers until
   Christmas

when your kid plays with the box
   instead of the toy

outdoor Christmas-decoration competitions

neighbors who complain about your
   pink lawn flamingos

when your toothbrush turns pink

ten-dollar-per-hour parking

movie trailers that show all the funny
scenes

airplane seats near the restrooms

looking like your driver's license
picture

very fast roaches

when everybody knows but you

when your team never wins the Pen-
nant

gritty sandwiches at the beach

seeing ugly people with gorgeous dates

when your steady says, "Can we just
be friends?"

when your significant other shaves her
legs with your razor

things called "o-rama" (e.g., Bowl-o-
rama)

those who think everything was better
years ago

things that really were better years ago

people who don't return your calls

a bee sting on the butt

flea bites around your ankles

going bald in high school

playing office politics

kids who pee in your pool

writers who dot their "i's" with little
   hearts

pranksters who push all the elevator
   buttons

prune juice that kicks in at an inoppor-
   tune time

"Do not back up; severe tire damage"
   signs

backhanded compliments

that Johnny Carson isn't on anymore

not dreaming in color

hearing your spouse and pet snore in
stereo

eggshell in the omelet

people who insult you, then say, "Just
kidding"

winning the booby prize

the useful psychic ability to bend
spoons mentally

the superior attitude of "natives"

when somebody has a "hissy fit"

the fact that Philadelphia-brand cream
cheese is made in Chicago

that Häagen-Dazs ice cream comes
   from New Jersey

that "plus tax" is always in small print

when your pita sandwich leaks all over
   your lap

plaque

that Superman isn't smart enough to
   invent an antidote to Kryptonite

that the Professor could build a radio
   from coconuts, but not a decent
   boat

sappy "Love is . . ." cartoons

getting gasoline on your clothes and
   smelling like a mechanic all day

people who hit the jackpot on their first
   coin

sneezing in your sleep and waking
   yourself up

being picked to be the magician's
    assistant

standing up when your foot's asleep

when the person whose name is tat-
    tooed on your body leaves

receiving a Chia Pet for your birthday

when your bottle of bubblesoap goes
    flat

people who ask how much you earn

open-casket funerals

wax fruit centerpieces

plastic slipcovers on beautiful couches

when your school isn't named on
snow-closure announcements

growing up where it never snows

sub-zero windchill factors

chattering teeth

shivering

heat waves in September

people who cleverly inquire, "Is it hot
enough for you?"

those who maintain, "It's not the heat,
it's the humidity"

misplacing the remote

products called "Mister Something"

finding out your new recipe tastes
awful in front of your dinner party

Sunday comics that haven't been
    funny in years

tripping on curled-up linoleum

people who wear sunglasses indoors

paying for insurance when you're
    accident-free

electronic wristwatches that don't
    tick—you can't tell if they're work-
    ing or not

waiting lines for the Ladies' Room, but
  not the Men's

when the phone rings while you're in
  the john

subway riders who fall asleep against
  you

people who say "passed away" instead
  of "died"

mail stamped "You may already be a
  winner!"

mail stamped "You are a winner!"

junk faxes

Fridays the 13th

when TV series are canceled without a
farewell episode

trying to find a house address on a dark
street

shirtsleeves that are just an inch too
long or too short.

when your hair dryer smells like burning hair

getting bitten by a petting-zoo animal

artificial intelligence

when everything grinds to a halt at
work because a computer goes
down

when your VCR runs out of tape and cuts off the end of the show

pitchers who take forever to throw the baseball

trying to find the start of a roll of clear tape

statement errors that are always in the bank's favor

how supermarkets put junk food at kids' eye-level

when friends tell you to get into ther-
apy because they are

when the library book you need to
complete your paper is checked
out

toenail clippings on the kitchen floor

when the pigeons sit on top of the fake
owl you put on the roof

people who clean out earwax with
their pinky in public

those useless "hints" in math word-
    problems

when you forget a dream as soon as
    you start to tell someone about it

when the police officer giving you a
    ticket is younger than you

getting stuck in a rut

slaves to fashion

spouses who shirk housework

hearing your favorite heavy-metal
    song as elevator music

cold stethoscopes

when the rough draft is better than the
    final version

Porsche drivers who pronounce it
    "porsh"

garbage trucks droning under your window at six A.M.

when the trash collectors strew your cans all over the street

unseen potholes

undercooked spaghetti

burned-out lights on the ceiling that are just out of your reach

people who can sleep through anything

top-forty disc jockeys

when a passing car backfires, causing
you to jump a foot into the air

cable outages during the big fight

street mimes

spoon players

subway symphonies

getting stuck at the top of the Ferris
wheel

when the cassette deck eats your tape

quitting smoking a dozen times

road tours by ancient rock groups

when kitty's been in the kid's sandbox
and left her calling card

bean-bag chairs

walking uphill in Birkenstocks

swimming in the ocean and getting
seaweed up your nose

jewelry that turns your skin green

movies starring children and sheep-
dogs

"water-saving" toilets you must flush
twice

knowing that insect parts are allowed
in peanut butter

that soap operas don't use organs for
background music anymore

Elvis sightings

long waxed mustaches

unsquelchable belches

earthquakes that strike when you're in
the bath

magazine renewal notices sent 9
months before the subscription
expires

when the coaster leaves a ring

Green Acres marathons on Nick at Nite

people who wear all-black clothing

yawners at your party

tourists who call San Francisco "Frisco"

trying to figure out the words to
    "Louie Louie"

zip-zip sounds when walking in cordu-
    roy pants

getting a bad clam

psychobabble

performance art

adults who have never had a cavity

alternate side of the street parking

early callers who invariably ask, "Did I
wake you?"

when someone peels your sunburn

incomprehensible slang

supermarket clerks who refuse to dou-
ble bag

marching behind the equestrian team

Boston accents

Star Trek I, III, and V

when valet parkers peel-out in your car

people who say, "Read my lips"

doctored tabloid photos

when someone puts empty ice cube
trays back in the freezer

getting only five McNuggets instead
of six

"No shirt, no shoes, no service" signs

hidden agendas

accordion players

"Lady of Spain" on accordion

infomercials

kids who think "the Big Bopper" was a
hamburger

waxing your bikini area

superstitious people

walking under a ladder

when you have to hold the TV's
antenna to get a clear picture

when commercials are twice as loud as
the TV program's volume level

when someone gives you "rabbit ears"
with their fingers in a photo

sneezes that build up but never deto-
nate

when letter carriers cram big
envelopes into your tiny mailbox

when charities send you "free" return-
address labels

never winning more than five bucks in
a lottery

the unappealing food at all-you-can-
eat restaurants

leaky diapers

when baby's first word is the pet's
name

squeaky windshield wipers

when you read the wrong horoscope,
but it applies anyway

when stores boost prices, then lower
them, and call it a "sale"

when restaurants call hamburger
"Salisbury Steak" and charge
more

people who are otherwise unimagina-
tive, except when it comes to lying

Norman Rockwell's paintings

throwing your back out

when the restroom has sandpaper-grade toilet paper

scented toilet paper

scratch-and-sniff spots scratched scentless

when a magazine's mailing label obscures the cover

losing a filling on vacation

graffiti spray painted on your car

hearing "Little Drummer Boy" fifty times during the holidays

the cast of Beverly Hills 90210

next-day packages that arrive two days later

when a fortune teller's shop burns down

when old flames let you know they're
    getting married

blue hair, except on clowns

being a glorified secretary

paper or plastic decisions

food servers who command you to
    "Enjoy your meal"

when the honeymoon ends

over-stuffed pencil sharpeners

when the "fresh" fish has freezer-burn

trying to use a solar-powered calculator at night

having to use three remotes to operate
your VCR

when half the cork stays in the bottle

people who get thumb prints on your
    photos

people who let the door slam in your
    face

springing ahead, falling back

flyers stuck under your windshield
    wipers

when the key breaks off in the lock

fault lines running through your
    pudding

people who say "uhh" a lot

people who never pick up the check

being the back half of a horse costume

when someone tells your kid there's no
Santa

Laundromat hogs who fill up all the
dryers

when a passing car splashes a filthy
puddle on you

soggy socks in school

thunderclaps at two A.M.

when your roommate does the laundry
and your underwear comes out
pink

having to rake leaves that came from a
neighbor's tree

the glances at your hair when you buy
dandruff shampoo

when someone calls on a speaker-
phone

people who take their time when
you're in a hurry

book reports on *Silas Marner*

teachers who want all homework typed

faded faxes

practical jokes

having your hand put in warm water
when you're asleep

people who write bogus answers on your crossword puzzle so it can't be solved

businesses that take more than two rings to answer

people who say "like" in every sentence

people who give out your unlisted number

when someone looks over your shoulder

hairsplitters and nitpickers

talking cars

being taken seriously all of the time

never being taken seriously

one-word names, like "Sting"

"not the real thing, but an incredible
    simulation"

why the phrase "sheep dip" is funny

people who say, "If you're so smart,
    how come you're not rich?"

high cholesterol

going to Monopoly jail

talking to someone with an unusually
 short attention span

when your pet theory gets shot full of
 holes

realizing that no decision is a decision
 in itself

when you're damned if you do,
 damned if you don't

that no UFOs have ever landed in
 Times Square, only in swamps
 and deserts

IQ tests that only measure how good
you are at taking IQ tests

being at the bottom of the pecking
order

being the Cheese in "Farmer in the
Dell"

limited-time offers

restaurants decorated with black velvet
paintings

when lettuce turns into a brown, semi-liquid mass in the refrigerator

car phones with answering machines

pro-athletes' salaries

having a hole in your sock when buying shoes

when the food's crummy and the portions are small

how lighting a cigarette makes the bus
    arrive

the first gray hair

that life is not fair

mini-malls

straws made so that you can't blow off
    the paper wrapper

gurus

when rich folks go slumming

people who don't wear socks with
     shoes

Rolls-Royces in any color but black

tattlers, hall monitors, teacher's pets

the class brain who throws off the
grading curve

going to the movies with your parents

being above or below the "average" in
height, weight, etc.

when the press gives emboldening
monikers to serial killers (e.g.,
"The Night Stalker")

packages that tick

$150 sneakers

waking up with your eyelids crusted
    shut

nutrition propaganda on bags of po-
    tato chips

discovering high-grade tape performs
    the same as standard

violin lessons for 3-year-olds

when bad things happen to good
people

when good things happen to bad
people

seeing records you paid full price for in
the close-out bin

when you laugh during breakfast and
milk comes out your nose

two-way mirrors in department store
changing rooms

imagining what your home's previous
owners probably did in the tub

being asked to murder errant insects

showers without tubs

people who put mustard on french
fries

Ed Sullivan impressions in the '90s

having a job like Chaplin's in *Modern Times*

card tricks that start, "Pick a card, any card"

people who won't reveal how a trick is done

radio shock-jocks

bumper stickers that tout "My other car is . . ."

when the coffee pot boils dry overnight

motorcycles that ride in between traffic
    lanes

when comic book super heroes are
    killed off

a seat under an air-conditioner vent in
    a chilly theater

the TV game show "Studs"

eternal optimists

when kitty claws the couch

a pet that bites the hand that feeds it

when drivers don't pull over for ambu-
lances

macaroni and cheese three nights in
a row

breaking up with your significant other
the day after your shrink goes on
vacation

spouses who toss Alka Seltzers in the
tub while you're in it

when someone knocks down your
house of cards

when your team loses by one point

when your sunny-side-up egg has a
broken yolk

forgetting how to tell the difference
   between the oral and rectal ther-
   mometers

sore winners

owning an extensive collection of
   8-track tapes

people who say, "It's just that simple"

settling down too young

aluminum Christmas trees

the mid-aisle moviegoer who goes for
    candy six times

overcast skies during a total eclipse

the bitter, metallic taste of your fingers
    after counting many pennies

that youth is wasted on the young

when the school dropout becomes rich
    and famous

when everyone is crazy but you

having only a "minor" credit card

forgetting how to do long division

that vein in fried chicken legs

when someone puts a "kick me" sign
   on your back

green McDonald's shakes on St.
   Paddy's Day

people who wear cowboy hats in the
   city

remaining forever five years old in
   your parents' eyes

that Dick Tracy only picks on de-
   formed criminals

hot dogs—ten to a pack; rolls—eight
   to a pack

when milk cartons with the best expi-
   ration date are hidden behind the
   old milk on the store shelf

homes with garden gnomes and lawn
   jockeys

people who stare

that instead of blowing things up with
   gunpowder, Mr. Wizard now
   performs tame experiments with
   computers

mailing your bills with "Love" stamps

receiving only 3 percent interest on your savings account

surfer slang (e.g., "Hey dude, surf's up")

books about dead cats

bagpipe music

going in a Porta-Potty

singing "Kum Ba Yah" around a campfire

pulling a groin muscle

handicapped parking spots at skating rinks

eating a rotten pistachio

trying to press the right remote control
button in the dark

having an allergic reaction to health
food

clear, non-foggy weather in San Francisco

forgetting to stamp an important letter

"Lot Full" signs

best-selling books and movies about
    vampires

goofy explanations for crop circles

when your PC catches a computer
    virus

people who seek the dubious achieve-
    ment of being the last name in the
    phone book

ocean-front homes with swimming
    pools

nearly breaking your neck on a freshly
    waxed wooden floor

when a snoop reads your diary

ethnic restaurants where you never see
    any ethnics dining

kite-flying competitions

people who say, "No can do"

dieters who assume a salad cancels out
   a sundae

the unreadably light goldenrod copy of
   multipart forms

blinking your eyes when your picture
   was taken

when they show hypodermic-needle
   injections on TV

an open-all-day zipper

being out of step in "The Hokey Pokey"

getting fruitcakes for Christmas

knocking your cup of coffee onto your desk

when your spouse gets amorous after eating Limburger cheese

drivers who turn to look at you every time they speak

never remembering if it's "feed a cold, starve a fever" or vice versa

taxi drivers with Ph.Ds

neighbors who use leaf-blowers

having to get tickets in advance to see a popular movie

mispronouncing a word you've never heard spoken, like "so-crates" for Socrates

reviews of new movies that give away
the ending

when you call out to someone you
think you know, but it's not them

yard sales blighting your block every
weekend

when your morning paper gets doused
by the lawn sprinklers

sardine cans with no key

sniffling concertgoers who just won't
    blow their noses

when your mom forgets your birthday

when someone answers the phone with
    "What do you want?"

going through a whole game of spin
    the bottle without getting kissed

frantically trying to find the public rest-
    rooms in a huge shopping mall

people who carve their names in trees

abandoned shopping carts in the check-out line

armchair psychologists who diagnose your personality flaws

people who base their personalities on TV characters

twenty-year reunions where no one has really changed

when someone plays "Connect-the-Dots" with the moles on your back

that

Mario Andretti, Ann Margaret, The Beach Boys, Candice Bergen, Cher, Chevy Chase, Joan Collins, Danny Devito, Michael Douglas, Linda Evans, Harrison Ford, Goldie Hawn, Mick Jagger, Paul McCartney, Bette Midler, Jack Nicholson, Dolly Parton, Linda Ronstadt, Diana Ross, Sylvester Stallone, Barbra Streisand, Tina Turner, and Raquel Welch

are all older than the President of the United States

"runny" fried eggs

directions on shampoo bottles to "Repeat"

kids who think long hair and tattoos
  are new

doormats that say "Get Lost"

talking with people who don't make
  eye contact

people who exclaim, "Fabulous!"

justifying your request for a pay raise
  to the boss

"I drive this way just to p*ss you off" bumper stickers

when motorcyclists make unnecessary "ba-room, ba-room" sounds at stoplights

when a kink renders your hula-hoop unusable

pool tables that are not level

how some people believe anything they see in print

after buying an expensive painting,
    being able to see the numbers

lazy jumping beans that will only roll
    over

wanna-be's

cold hot dogs

days without free time

the disgusting noise made by nearly
empty squeeze-bottles of ketchup

ant-like conformity

those who pronounce coupon "kew-
pon"

polka dances

working the graveyard shift

people who worry that someone,
somewhere, is having a great time

people who knew what they wanted to
be by the time they were ten

searching for intelligent life in space
when Earth could use some

oil company ads about their concern
for the fragile ecology

paying more for extra fat and chemi-
cals in premium ice cream

parents who nagged you to eat everything on your plate and now think
  you should diet

that no license is required to become a
  parent

when you bring home half the beach in
  your shoes

when the merry-go-round breaks down

that the Peace symbol now means
  "Mercedes"

that ignorance isn't painful

writer's block

people who wash dishes before putting
    them in the dishwasher

when your mom uses spit to wash off
    your face

teenagers who neck in public

when brothers/sisters look through
your private things

a Special News Bulletin in the middle
of your favorite TV show

that pocket-size piece of steak you're
served on airlines

when your dog wants to go out at
three A.M.

finding exactly what you're looking for
in a store, and discovering you're
out of money

when the only ATM around is out of
order

getting no response when you answer
an ad in the personals

having to work overtime on the night
that you have your first date in 2
years

gas stations that don't have signs telling
you whether to "Pump First" or
"Pay First"

when you go to see the movie voted
"Best Picture" and loathe it

getting a bill for clothing you paid
   cash for

rain on your day off

sunny beach weather on a workday

credit card finance charges

"user-unfriendly" computers

trying to get burrs out of the dog's fur

1-900 phone line charges

losing someone's unlisted phone number

the last day of vacation

the first day back at school after summer vacation

when the boss just laughs at you after
    you ask for a raise

having to buy a whole compact disc to
    get the one song you want

finding out you are a blonde when all
    along you thought you were light-
    brown-headed

Mothers who insist that orange and
    purple match and get upset when
    you don't wear them together

people who enter dance contests but
    have two left feet

people who say, "That was then, this is
   now"

having to memorize anything

stapling your finger

people with shag hairstyles and side-
   burns

being called an unflattering name and
   knowing it's true

people who say, "You're so imma-
ture!"

seeded grapes

thong underwear

moon boots

losing an hour's sleep because of day-
light saving time

turning a curve and all your groceries
in the trunk fall out of the sack,
squash each other, and leak every-
where

when somebody waters down the
shampoo and conditioner to
"stretch" them

genuine imitation leather

loving someone who doesn't know you
exist

getting stuck in the mud

running out of gas in the middle of
    nowhere

when your car breaks down in a fire-
    bombed neighborhood

mind-numbingly boring college courses
    such as Medieval English Lit.

failing a class you really thought you
    were doing well in

when you can't use your new calcula-
    tor because batteries aren't in-
    cluded

country music singers who speak with
a "twang"

being confined to a seat belt by law

only getting two hours of sleep the
night before finals

when the TV news is just one depres-
sing story after another

insurance companies that raise rates
annually

getting the first scratch on a new car

people who can eat all they want and
stay slim

people who complain they're having a
hard time putting on weight

people who cut in line and those who
sheepishly allow them to get away
with it

interest on bank loans at rates formerly
charged by loan sharks

advertisements that say you can make
$300 a week mailing letters

membership fees

when the only cable company serving
your area stinks

Congress voting to give themselves a
raise

bosses who take credit for your ideas

when your company merges and goes
through "restructuring"

people who threaten to sue at the drop
of a hat

having to paint your condo the same
color as everyone else's

painting a light color over a dark color

drivers who "burn rubber" whenever
the light turns green

people who own a four-wheel-drive
truck with a lift kit and big tires,
but never take it off-road

walky-talky pedestrians with cellular
  phones

two-lane highways

walking on a narrow bridge when a
  huge truck is coming at you

finding yourself caring if Miss Green-
  land will win the Miss Universe
  beauty contest

gas prices ending in "9/10" of a cent,
  instead of a round number

having to learn useless things, like how to find a square root

when your dog's Christmas stocking is bigger than yours

getting a run in new pantyhose 5 minutes after you put them on

post-Christmas depression

baby-sitting for an eight-year-old know-it-all

long-haired dogs that smell

having an infinite number of things to
    be p*ssed about

being a female who happens to be in a
    bad mood and having someone
    assume that it's "that time of the
    month" again

people who say, "Oh, you don't really
    mean that," when you vow to love
    them forever

when people expect you to call them
    because they want to talk to you

customers with smelly feet when you work in a shoestore

hearing from your lawyer only when a bill is due

when you buy a juice box and no straw comes with it

speakers who think you're too dense to grasp meanings, i.e., "Ya see what I mean? . . . Ya follow what I'm sayin'?"

dealership names on car trunks

walking alongside someone wearing an
"I'm With Stupid" T-shirt

the noise and diesel fumes of buses

ATM messages that imply you're trying to rob the bank when the machine is simply out of cash

change for the sake of change

being stuck behind anything but a pas-
senger car in traffic

making two trips to the pharmacy to
get a prescription filled correctly

being in the wrong career field for
years before you realize it

chewing gum in ashtrays

getting a wire bra out of the washer or
dryer with the wire all twisted

wanting to return something that you
threw away the receipt for

being carded at bars after you've
turned twenty-one

phone calls at nine A.M. when you got
to bed at five A.M.

when all of your dishes are in the dishwasher

when the supermarket has every ingre-
dient for your special carrot stew,
except carrots

people who say they'll call back, but
never do

trying to get your new hairstyle to look
the way the hairdresser got it to
look

getting your hair stuck in the blow-
dryer

getting flowers and not having a vase
to put them in

people who talk too fast when they
leave a phone number on your answering machine

forgetting your ATM card code

bars that charge $4.25 for a 12-oz.
  beer

getting to the store and forgetting what
  you went there for

The Columbia House Record Club

seeing cats kill things

when the page that you're tearing off a
  pad rips down the middle

your fine china cups permanently
stained purple by Kool-Aid

accidentally recording over the videotape of your once-in-a-lifetime trip

leaky aquariums

running out of stamps

Dr. Seuss's dying

children who don't cry when Bambi's
    mother dies

accidentally addressing an envelope
    upside down

couples with their multiple children
    who have all day to walk in front
    of you at the mall

skirts that ride up your legs more and
    more as you walk down the hall

the mysterious source of all the dust in
    your home

teachers who grade on a curve

the hundreds of advertisements in
    good magazines

malls at Christmas time

seeing a reflection in a window and
    thinking "What a porker" before
    recognizing yourself

Bob Hope specials

mega-developers who destroy your
favorite scenic spot and put in
a gaudy shopping center and a
thousand condos

hair in your food

reckless cab drivers who give you white
knuckles

when you shout into a cave and there's
no echo

spouses who tell guests that you drool
in your sleep

when there's nothing good to eat in the
house

people who always fidget with something

dogs who stick their noses between
your legs

people who wear a beret trying to look
"artsy"

bird droppings in the fireplace

furiously spraying a large insect only to have it escape, while your room smells like bug spray for days

people who take off their shirts in public and gross everyone out

people who say, "At least it will grow out" after you get a really bad haircut

snotty cosmetic-counter salespeople

when the waitress asks, "How is everything?" while your mouth is stuffed

waking up in the middle of a good
   dream

watery stuff that comes out of ketchup
   and mustard bottles

clipping coupons and then forgetting
   to take them out when you reach
   the cash register

people who give confusing directions
   and then finish with, "You can't
   miss it!"

Brady Bunch reunion shows

vending machines that release the coffee before the cup comes down

summer colds that don't go away until
late fall

kumquat jelly donuts

people who wear sandals and socks

Mikhail Gorbachev's birthmark

articles that list Warren Beatty's con-
quests

Sonny talking about Cher or Cher
talking about Sonny

remakes of oldies you didn't like the
first time around

when cars belch smoke but somehow
pass the state's emissions check

breaking a shoelace

finding the collar on the one-hundred-dollar designer shirt you've only worn once is now too tight to button

getting crumpled, dirty, or torn dollar bills as change from a cashier

being behind someone in the check-out line who presents an unpriced item that needs to be price checked

running out of windshield-washer fluid

when Mom gives you two ties and you wear one and she says, "What's the matter, don't you like the other one?"

spilling mustard on your freshly washed shirt

getting a busy signal when you call the phone company

when your landlord leaves a mess behind after fixing the toilet

trying to fit a plug in an outlet in the dark

"No turn on red" signs

rude police officers

kids with raging hormones during
    puberty

lukewarm pizza delivered 29 minutes
    after ordering

trying to remove a smudge that's on
    the other side of the glass when
    washing windows

when people move and don't leave a
    forwarding address

packaged ketchup that covers only about two of your french fries

blower-type hand dryers and no paper towels

stores that run out of specials the first day

when someone puts food in the sink but doesn't run the disposal

people who say, "I'm sorry," but you know they aren't

when you fix a special dinner and
    someone says, "This would be bet-
    ter if . . ."

people who think they are never wrong

when you barely miss the traffic light

cars that take up two parking spaces

change machines that only give you
    tokens

when there's not enough water pres-
   sure in a shower to wash the shampoo out of your hair

fortuneless fortune cookies

people who rattle pans/grind coffee/
   wash dishes/rumple paper on the
   other end of the phone

when they don't fill pill bottles to
   the top

when the toilet seat is left up

missing with the mascara and getting it
in your eye

when your favorite T-shirt is ready to
be a dust rag

popcorn stuck in your teeth

cars going the wrong way against you
on a one-way street that wait for
you to move over

getting Q-tip fuzz in your eye

when dry cleaners destroy your clothes

store clerks who don't say "thank you"
    for your purchase

cheap one-ply hotel toilet paper

cheap hotel facial tissue

slipping on the bathroom floor

plastic price tags on clothes that leave
a hole

when the clerk forgets to take the sen-
sor tags off your new clothes

when your spouse steals all the covers

when your favorite scent/eye shadow,
etc., is discontinued

doctors who keep you waiting an hour,
then see you for only three minutes

people who chew with their mouth
   open

people who comb their hair at the
   table

people who won't take your calls

when you rush to a movie and find that
   you read the wrong time in the
   paper

cooks with dirt under their fingernails

people who park too close and always
bang your car door

apartment neighbors who blast their
stereo

when you're on your way to an important meeting and your flight's
delayed

people who say "wee" instead of
"little"

radio stations that say "We play 52
minutes of music," but really play
52 minutes of talk and commercials

people who don't look where they're
    going while walking

trying to read a wet newspaper

fund-raising bake sales where most of
    the goodies are store-bought

candy stores that charge 3 cents for
    samples

guests who bring a bag of potato chips
    to a Bar-B-Q and proceed to eat
    $20.00 worth of food

theaters that won't take cash but charge to process credit card purchases

turning fifty and being told how wonderful getting older is

seeing a good sale, being asked out for lunch, or any other minor emergency two days before payday

teachers who assign expensive and complex projects to do at home, like a home-made solar power generator

when you remember 5 minutes after it's over that your favorite TV program or movie was on

real-estate salespeople

when the motel forgets your incredibly
important wake-up call

the year that you buy your swimming
pool turns out to be the wettest
and coldest on record

finding out that you spend more time
cleaning your pool than swimming
in it

people who suck their teeth after a
meal

when the cap breaks off the shampoo
    bottle in your suitcase

going to a job interview and being told
    they'll let you know in a few days,
    and never hearing from them

a 48-hour lay-off notice after being
    told the lay-off won't affect you

rain on the 4th of July

after throwing out the stray sock
    you've been holding onto for 6
    months, you find the matching
    sock

getting to the beach and noticing that
you missed one patch of hair when
you shaved your legs

ordering something from a shopping
channel that looked great on TV,
but is a piece of junk when you
get it

finding out something you sold at a
yard sale last year for $1.00 is now
a very valuable collector's item

looking all over town and not being
able to find the only toy your child
wants for Christmas

shoes that felt good when you bought
  them, but kill your feet the first
  time you wear them

when you're buying lipstick, having
  the clerk ask if you would be inter-
  ested in wrinkle cream for your
  eyes

spray cans that don't work

no phone books at public phones

loaning your lighter to someone and
  later realizing they didn't give it
  back

forgetting to take out the garbage on
garbage day

getting a flimsy excuse when you ask a
favor of someone to whom you've
been very generous

being depressed over missing part 2 of
a 2-part TV movie

not remembering how to do eighth-
grade math when your child needs
help with his homework

clerks who follow you around as if
you're a shoplifter, but who are
never around when you need them

reading a good magazine article in a doctor's office, only to find someone has ripped out the last page

getting cut off after your doctor's office puts you on hold for 10 minutes

discovering after you get home that you were charged regular price for a sale item

when someone sees an old picture of you and says, "My, you've changed," and nothing else

after spending $400.00 on a new appliance, having to put a stamp on the warranty card when rich people win lotteries

waiting at home all day for repair people who don't show up

paying for air for your tires

when your colored underwear shows
through your white pants

advertisements that claim "Simply the
best!"

rich people who are cheap

store aisles too narrow for your cart to
    get through

people who say, "It's your responsibil-
    ity!" when it isn't

unwrapped free food samples

unfilleted fish

receiving a single cheap gift from an entire family for whom you bought individual gifts

people who tell you that you've gained weight, as if you didn't know it

tuna fish that tastes fishy

work-out freaks who talk constantly about exercising

people who discuss the scarier aspects of their love lives on TV talk shows

having to call in to work sick on a
    Monday or Friday when you are
    really sick

stores that display "Come in, we're
    open" signs when they're closed

when the caller hangs up just as you
    answer the phone

wrong-number callers who hang up
    without apologizing

waiting for white-out to dry

when you forget your watch and keep
checking your wrist all day long

staplers that don't work

used diapers discarded in parking lots

edited-for-television movies

people who think bodily noises are
deliriously funny

the cockroach stampede when you
flick on the lights

when people wear see-through shirts
without an undershirt

going swimming in a lake and encoun-
tering something dead and rotting

when a hornet gets into the house and
spends the day bouncing off the
ceiling

the person growing roots in front of
whatever it is you want in the gro-
cery store

people who think children covering
themselves with food are adorable

people who borrow your pencil, and
then return it covered with teeth
marks

long or rolled-up sleeves that ride up to
your armpits when you put on a
jacket

getting a mouse out of a sprung trap

tailgaters who plow into your car and
then sue you for injuries

when you've just spent tons of money
on a new outfit and you see someone else wearing it

when nail polish is goopy

when you set your alarm for eight P.M.
instead of eight A.M.

going to work to pick up your paycheck and having them tell you it
was just sent out in the mail

bringing home Chinese food and finding out there is no sweet 'n' sour
sauce

broken glass in the sand at the beach

people who ask, "Are you my friend?" when you can't stand them

arguing over which way the toilet paper should be hung on the dispenser

people who expend more energy trying to get out of a task than it would take to simply do it

teenagers who think they are smarter than their parents

teenagers who ARE smarter than their parents

pay raises lower than the rate of inflation

the smell of public restrooms

getting saltwater up your nose at the beach

discovering that you forgot to put the answering machine on AFTER you return from a 2-week vacation

when the Saran Wrap sticks to itself
    after you pull it out

when you say no, but are subsequently
    convinced to say yes

people who let their dog jump on you

wafer-thin hotel pillows

rotten pumpkins all black and fuzzy

a beer-bellied man in a bikini bathing
   suit

people who wipe toothpaste off on the
   hand towels

being told to "act your age"

being very ticklish and everyone knowing it

people who laugh like hyenas

walking into a glass door

pee on the toilet seat

crumbly deodorant

mosquito bites in the wintertime

a beehive over the front door

the demise of full-service stations

when the wax from a cardboard milk
carton falls into your cup

when your younger sibling gets the pet
you always wanted

when something falls into the toilet
and you have to fish it out with
your hand

being the shortest player on the basketball team

crank calls

warm soda

not winning at the carnival games

ripping a week-old Band-Aid off your
    hairy leg

hand-scrubbing dirty underwear

when your wedding ring goes down
   the bathroom drain

school on a hot, 90-degree day

sharing a room with your brother or
   sister

people who laugh for no reason

cleaning under the rim of an oval toilet

soup-slurpers

people who go in the "out" door

when your mom makes you give back
a twenty-dollar bill someone gave
you for your birthday

getting a present in a big box and most
of it is just tissue paper

when the next rest area is 20 miles
away

watching the bus pass by after you wait
a long time at the bus stop

when you buy five packs of baseball
cards and you already have every
single one

when everyone is cheering for you to
catch a pass at a football game,
and you miss it

when someone says something good
about you, but then apologizes for
thinking you were someone else

teachers who read your grade out loud
in class when you fail a test

vending machines that won't take your dollar because it's a little wrinkled

people who devour a whole box of mallowmars and then insist, "I didn't eat all of them"

multi-page application forms for fast-food jobs

magazines that don't publish your letters

magazines that do publish your letter, but with the best part edited out

being the ninth caller at a radio station
when the tenth caller will be the
winner

waiting 3 years for your favorite
group's next album

obviously staged entries on "America's
Funniest Home Videos"

local news that only talks about home-
town sports teams

being fooled by those Energizer-bunny
ads on TV

the World League of American
    Football

when radio stations play the same stu-
    pid song more than once an hour

five-year-olds who beat you at video
    games

infant black belts

parents who can't stop bragging

parents who say "my Bobby" instead
    of just "Bobby"

bad calls in a crucial game

group projects in a class in which you
    don't know anybody

teacher's pets

sappy endings

when a CD you just bought skips

not being able to pick your nose in
public

when players make 3 million dollars a
year right out of college

TVs with no remote control

telephones with a dial instead of push
buttons

people who don't swear

losing chess to a computer

when they forget to send your magazine one month

when other people take credit for
something you said

actors turned directors

actors turned singers

when junk mail misspells your name

when all the good CDs are released in
the same month and you can't afford them all at once

people who start their sentences,
"Well, back home . . ."

when your favorite singer collaborates
with someone you hate

the last 15 minutes of the work day

Sam Donaldson's eyebrows

politically charged acceptance speeches
at entertainment awards shows

that Air Jordans don't make you a better basketball player

losing a phone number because you
can't find the piece of paper you
wrote it on

the doctor saying, "Let's try this . . ."

toothaches on holidays or weekends

emergencies always happening when
the doctor is not in

"Somebody moved it. I left it right
there"

having to watch the bad TV program
selected by your now-dozing
spouse

going to the doctor's and finding out
your scale reads 10 pounds too low

contractors who never finish a job by
the promised date

the same news at five and six P.M., and
at ten and eleven P.M.

water on the basement floor

kids with expensive toys laying them
aside to play with pots and pans

people who complain about a driver's
   actions based on the driver's sex,
   color, or nationality

the neighbor's cat digging in your
   garden

people in passing cars who throw
   empty cans into your yard

looking feverishly for a parking spot,
   thinking you found one, but
   there's a compact car in it

IRS "E-Z" forms

gas pains

"Out of Service" signs

the comment, "We need to talk"

the comment, "Talk to my lawyer"

chalkboard screech

dull speakers

bumping into your ex

finding a boot on your car tire

tests of the Emergency Broadcast
    System

drinking fountains that squirt only the
    barest thread of water

over-salted food

a seat behind a pole at a concert

meetings where nothing meaningful is
said or accomplished

the sounds of a dentist's office

"Occupied" signs

forgetting your password

the comment, "I think I'm pregnant"

not qualifying for the "short form"

stores that take every credit card but yours

having to wait for the best books to come out in paperback

stuck jar lids

real fur coats

people who always ask you to do some
    of their work

the smell of over-ripe bananas

the smudgy carbon paper you get back
    with your credit card receipt

strong perfume

discovering a seat is wet after you sit
down

air "freshener" odor

the sound of screeching tires getting
closer and louder

being questioned about an article
you've only half read

emergency vehicles that use their lights
   and sirens just to go through a red
   light, and then turn them off

bug smears on the windshield

car service "estimates"

cheap arcade prizes

bathtub rings

hearing "Life begins at forty" when you're only twenty

recorded phone solicitations

imported fruits and vegetables at the local Farmer's Market

people who sneeze on you

sticky door knobs

the question: "Have you put on a few
  pounds?"

not sleeping in your own bed

the ill effects antibiotics have on your
  stomach

living next door to people who don't
  take care of their yard

heart-stopping surprises when you're
  desperate for calm

stuck elevators

an ice cube dropped down your back

new clothes that need ironing

amateur artwork

15-minute parking meters

discovering a fire hydrant just when you thought you found a parking spot

bus stations that haven't been redecorated since 1945

knowing it's 364 days until your next birthday

being told by the "Fashion Police" that you're not color coordinated

barbed wire

bicycle couriers

claims of "legitimacy" by pro wrestlers

meter monitors

stone chips on the windshield

following trucks dropping gravel

a "click, click, click" sound when you
turn the ignition key

the boss's offspring

"courteous" dates who walk five feet in
front of you when entering and
leaving a restaurant

people who tell "bartender jokes"
while they wait for a drink

people who say, "I don't know, I only
work here"

people who say "might" or "maybe" instead of saying "no"

the smell of a pet that passes noiseless gas

having to call 1-900 numbers to find out what you won

being the third out on a team when the bases are loaded

when you can't stop snickering after everyone else has stopped laughing

when you can't tune in a good radio
   station just right

people who say, "Excuse you"

drivers who park sideways or at an
   angle in a normal parking spot

when you wake up on Sunday and
   think it's Monday

trying to mow grass that should have
   been mowed a week ago

when your favorite magazine comes in the mail looking like it's been through a hurricane

putting away the lawn mower and then noticing that you missed a spot

when you can't get your contact lens in

when you cut your finger on the Band-Aid box

when a friend overestimates your interest in a conversation

trying to put socks on wet feet

lying in the sun all day and not getting
a tan

when restaurants don't put spoons on
the table

when you must lie down to zip up your
jeans

paper cuts on your lip from licking envelopes

trying to scratch an itch on your foot
through your shoe

cleaning services that steal

when a new bag of potato chips is filled
halfway

when you put something down and
come back and it's not there

when you don't "get" jokes

burning your hand every time you bake cookies

losing your train of thought when you're in the middle of saying something important

feeling incredibly dirty and not having time to take a shower

personalized license plates that only their owner can decipher

400-pound gym teachers

500-pound health teachers

pants that aren't pulled up all the way

pants that are pulled up above the waist

quiz-show hosts who act as if they'd know the answers even if they weren't right in front of them

when your cable system carries three home-shopping channels

biting into a jalepeño pepper by accident

getting ready to load the dishwasher and finding it full of clean dishes

joggers running four abreast on the street

feeling for your car keys in a huge purse

when someone asks you if you're pregnant and you're not

getting lemon juice in paper cuts

Siskel and Ebert

the loud tape recorder click when the relaxation tape ends

always picking the slowest line at the ski lift

the reassuring announcement that you can use your airplane seat as a flotation device

when your mate always blurts out the
Wheel of Fortune answer just before
you get it

guests who rest their feet on your coffee table

having to put your seat back in the
upright position

when you've finally gotten to sleep and
your mate asks, "Are you asleep
yet?"

first names that end in "i"

old mushrooms that moosh when you
try to slice them

the person who always orders the most
expensive dinner when you're
splitting the check

a half-inch-wide space on forms for
your complete address

not seeing the one red sock in the white
wash load

wine in a box

family Christmas letters detailing who
died, divorced, etc., in the last year

split ends

polyester suits

overdue video fines

the same commercial twice in a row

when it's not bright enough for sunglasses but too bright without
them

high-beam car lights shining in your
car's side and rearview mirrors

people who send cheap gifts in fake
Tiffany boxes

pizza commercials at seven A.M.

chicken stock scum

people with "perfect" hair

your mate trying to get comfortable in
your water bed

a total eclipse of the sun except in your
part of the country

people who start sentences with "Her
and I"

whiskers in the sink after your mate
cleans the razor

people who start sentences with "Now
   don't take this the wrong way,
   but . . ."

fifty-one cards in a deck

pizza gunk under your fingernails

trying to tighten the screw on your eye-
   glasses but not being able to see
   without your glasses on

a quart of cellophane-wrapped straw-
   berries with bright red ones on
   top and hard green ones on the
   bottom

when the tongue of your tennis shoes
keeps slipping to the side

when someone with big hair sits in
front of you in a theater

people who know the punch line but
forget the rest of the joke

when wet dogs shake themselves near
you

itchy ear drums

plants that die two days after you get
   them home

the fish in the tank that eats all the
   other fish

the loose wire in your car radio

writers who don't know where to put
   modifying phrases

getting caught napping

when someone sees you yanking up
   your nylons or socks

when the experts don't know what's
   wrong

when you cook a nice dinner and the
   first word out of the kids' mouths is
   "UGH"

when the school bus forgets to pick up
   the kids

when children smell their dinner to de-
   termine if they will eat it

when you're stuck in the "Exact Change" lane without exact change

sap on Christmas trees

people who swim in the ocean in the winter

people who interrupt your conversation with questions like "What?" and "Who?"

realizing that there's still 30 minutes left in math class

people who think they have a snow-
ball's chance in hell of winning the
Publisher's Clearing House contest

injuries sustained while trying to prop
up the Christmas tree

ads for albums that list a few songs
"and many more"

the never-ending supply of toupee gags

being a father who is too small to wear
men's clothing

clothing manufacturers who think all
stripes on sportswear for large
people should be horizontal

clothing without pockets

VCRs that don't let you adjust the
tracking with the remote control

People who say, "Somebody ought to
do something about . . ."

two-volume biographies

Shakespeare academics

wasting 2 hours of your life by watching a PBS documentary on the
love life of a squid

when you're feeling ill and someone
says, "But you don't *look* sick"

waiting an hour to get a bad 5-minute
haircut

smokers who claim, "I can quit any-
time I want"

being a game show runner-up and
    winning a lifetime supply of Rice-
    a-Roni

a five-year-old with a pacifier

falling off the "fast track"

ants at your picnic

lines to get gas

talking to someone with a nose-ring
and trying not to stare at it

trying to read your digital watch in the
dark

Hair Club for Men advertisements
on TV

wearing a "flesh-toned" Band-Aid
when your skin isn't

the Elvis stamp

people who are sure "Big Bands" will
come back someday

sharp downturns in the economy

jackhammers

bullhorns

collections of ceramic frogs

when people vent their spleen all
    over you

kids who divorce their parents

cowchip-tossing contests

having to look busy at work

all the money that was spent to go to
    the moon and bring back some
    rocks

dusty books

days the world is predicted to end, and
    it doesn't

creeping couchpotatoism

moving when Simon didn't say

where your kids learn those clever dit-
    ties about beans

owning a 500-tape video library, on
   Beta

when a kid is told the technical reason
   for a rainbow

TV screens measured diagonally to
   make you think they're bigger

rental stores with 10,000 movies, except the one you're dying to see
   tonight

endless presidential press conferences

pizza still frozen in the center

when golf is called a sport

waxy yellow buildup on your linoleum

unwanted attention from sailors

the song, "I'm Looking Over My Dead
Dog, Rover"

being given a gold retirement watch
for thirty-five years of work

tricycle thieves

getting "the willies"

an attack of the "heebie-jeebies"

calculator dependency

oatbran candy bars

when you walk across a carpet, touch a
doorknob, and get a shock

having no "Plan B"

wearing orange and black clothes on
any day EXCEPT Halloween

when you wear a black suit, and someone asks "Who died?"

having 110 cable channels when there's nothing worth watching

"Snappy," the crazed, aggressive duck at the pond

when the fun-park ride starts up, the person who always says, "H-e-r-e we go!"

spending any time wondering if Elvis is alive

when you blurt an answer to a rhetorical question

looking up into the night sky and being
able to count only a dozen stars

blue food (e.g., Jell-O, corn chips, etc.)

that other, faster lane

offers that sound too good to be true,
and are

when someone becomes too sophis-
ticated to own a rubber chicken

being told something unfair is "company policy"

when people advise you, "Don't quit
   your day job"

while eating a burger, finding yourself
   thinking about the cow that the
   meat came from

"working" on a relationship

gas guzzlers

those who believe that bigger is better

learning your weather forecaster isn't really a meteorologist

"power"-prefixing quite ordinary activities, like lunch

Spandex bicycle-riding outfits

over-achievers

smelling the smoke wafting from your
dentist's drill

hot dogs made from turkey meat

people who stumble to the tune of a
different flutist

the song "It's a Small World" burned
into your brain

the fact that "I Love Lucy" is playing
somewhere in the world every
hour

flickering fluorescent lights

buying your first station wagon

scraping your knuckles on the cheese
   grater

inheriting your family's dysfunctions

smarter-than-average bears

kids who use magnifying glasses to fry
ants

worker-motivation posters

the appliance that fixes itself when the
repairman comes

being accused of having a "bad attitude"

sneezing more than three times in
public

people who laugh "Har-har-har!"

kids who say the #&*@$!!-darndest
    things

allegedly humorous movies advertised
    as "zany"

whisker burn

speed-dialing a wrong number

being told to stay inside the coloring
    book's lines

wondering if you are what you eat

office size as a measurement of success

flowers that bloom unseen

$3.00 comic books

being damned with faint praise

lax truth-in-advertising laws that allow
things like X-ray Specs and Sea
Monkeys to stay on the market

unwittingly eating a chocolate-covered
grasshopper

the crowd-stopping appeal of "Human
Mannequins"

a clown in normal-size shoes

why anyone would think a clam is
    happy

dogs wearing bandannas

after breathing helium, your voice not
    returning to normal

when someone chews all your pens

pet-to-pet greeting cards

self-appointed kings (e.g., The King of Pop; The Carpet King; The Burger King, etc.)

classes in humor analysis

when "Cajun-blackened" means "burned"

when the most creative kid is called the "class clown"

big bearded guys who see you when you're sleeping, know if you're awake, been bad or good, etc.

being cursed by a gypsy cab driver

discovering that vanishing cream
doesn't really turn you invisible

societal norms

applying the word "genius" to both
Einstein and Jerry Lewis

chunk-style Jell-O

people who reel off their pet peeves

seeing a roach in an award-winning
restaurant

feeling squeamish about riding a roller
coaster

scientists using the Hubbell Space Tel-
escope to watch people undressing
on earth

making snow angels in the yellow snow

junkfood-eating reptile super heroes

when your favorite song tops a critic's
    "Ten-Worst" list

Montezuma's revenge

when your mom throws away your col-
    lection of comic books

when your parents start liking your
    music

pencils without erasers

hearing "oops" in an operating room

riding the bumper cars unscathed

going to 31 Flavors, ordering vanilla

tourists eating at McDonald's in
Tokyo

the admonition to "never put anything in your ear except your elbow"

the power of a white coat to confer scientific credibility upon the wearer

those who answer the phone "Yellow?"

weight losses equivalent to a pimple off a watermelon

being unable to remember your "first time," or the last time

Clinton's campaign promises

Chelsea jokes

people who don't vote and then bitch
for four years

people who scratch their armpits in
public

belching contests

dogs walked without a leash

bus riders who fumble for change after
boarding the bus

kids who scream "You can't make
me!"

someone wearing a fur coat in a pet
store

when your roommate drinks your last
can of soda

the pale and sickly pallor of health food
store employees

finding soggy, shredded money in the
washing machine

singers who forget the words to the
National Anthem at ball games

not understanding most modern
poetry

people who pretend they're listening
when you're speaking

Christmas carolers singing off-key

waking up in a cold sweat

being stood up by a date

buying a $2,000 computer and using it
just to balance a checkbook

losing face

forgetting to take your comb on a
windy day

middle-age spread

running out of charcoal-lighter fluid

hunters who use semi-automatic
weapons

fishermen who use electronic fish-
tracking equipment

people who slap you on the back when
    you're sunburned

when executives of nearly bankrupt
    corporations receive huge salaries
    and bonuses

"golden parachutes"

the return of bellbottoms

buying "crystal" cola that you mistook
    for 7-Up

being unable to afford a home like
your parents owned

naughty news shows during TV
"sweeps week"

airline "near misses"

blueberry-flecked muffins

mystery-meat sandwiches

chicken-feet soup

how a watched pot never boils

realizing that the cure for aging will
probably be discovered when
you're eighty

counting holes in ceiling tiles to
counter boredom

people who wear white shoes and a
matching white belt

being the last kid on the block to get
   something new

endlessly pursuing slenderness

people who pronounce "really" as
   "rilly"

when intelligent people rent Rambo
   movies

Michael Jackson's Kafka-esque meta-
   morphosis

bosses who want you to call problems
     "opportunities"

yeast infections

when a tomato soup commercial fol-
     lows a bloody stabbing on a TV
     crime show

ultimatums

missing your life's calling

thorns on greenhouse-grown roses

buy-read-heed-or-don't-succeed   self-
    help books

people who say "nucular"

being an assistant to an assistant

packets of airline peanuts that you
    have to use your teeth to tear open

dental-floss bikinis for $49.95

when your speech receives just a smat-
tering of polite applause

when "all of the above" is the correct
answer

seagulls that target your car with pin-
point accuracy

people who teach kids to swim by toss-
ing them in the deep end

finding your mate's nailclippings in
  bed

when your potatoes start to sprout

fish served with the head still on

celebrity mobsters

seeking solace in week-old cheesecake
  at two in the morning

when your favorite rock star starts
    playing Vegas

the cheezy lounge singer who ruins
    your parents' golden anniversary
    party

parrots with ear-splitting squawks

aerosol-can cheese

people with a sick sense of humor who
    are funny as hell

people flaunting hickeys

brain teasers that you can't solve without secretly looking up the answer

sequels